0

plant parts

Leaves

Melanie Waldron

Raintree is an imprint of Capstone Global Library Limited, a company incorporated in England and Wales having its registered office at 7 Pilgrim Street, London, EC4V 6LB – Registered company number: 6695582

www.raintreepublishers.co.uk
myorders@raintreepublishers.co.uk

Edited by Sian Smith and Adrian Vigliano
Designed by Cynthia Akiyoshi
Original illustrations © HL Studios
Illustrated by HL Studios
Picture research by Mica Brancic
Originated by Capstone Global Library Ltd
Printed in China by CTPS

ISBN 978 1 406 27478 3
17 16 15 14 13
10 9 8 7 6 5 4 3 2 1

British Library Cataloguing in Publication Data
Waldron, Melanie
Leaves (Plant parts)
A full catalogue record for this book is available from the British Library.

Acknowledgements
We would like to thank the following for permission to reproduce photographs: Alamy p. 9 (© Plantography); Capstone Publishers pp. 10, 11, 20, 21 (© Karon Dubke); Naturepl.com pp. 12 (© Nick Garbutt), 19 (© Visuals Unlimited), 23 (© George McCarthy), 25, 27 (© Chris Mattison); Shutterstock pp. 4 (© Ivalin), 5 (© Pal Teravagimov), 6 (© Richard Griffin), 7 (© Timothy Michael Morgan), 13 (© Stephen VanHorn), 14 (© Anna Subbotina), 14 (© Piotr Malczyk), 15 (© fajno), 17 (© Elliotte Rusty Harold), 19 (© joannawnuk), 24 (© Dr. Morley Read), 25 (© Alessandro Colle), 26 (© Alan49), 28 (© Jelle vd Wolf), 16 bottom (© zhu difeng), 16top (© vladis.studio), 22 main (© KA Photography KEVM111), 22 top (© Artens), 29 bottom (© Anna Fotyma), 29 top (© Kamonrat), imprint page (© sauletas), title page (© Carlos Caetano).

Cover photograph reproduced with permission of Shutterstock (© Carlos Caetano).

We would like to thank Michael Bright for his invaluable help in the preparation of this book.

Contents

Some words are shown in bold, **like this**. You can find out what they mean by looking in the glossary.

A green world

If you looked at Earth from space, you would see huge areas of green covering the land. Only areas such as the huge sandy deserts and the icy North and South poles are not green. Now take a look outside. You will probably see some green plants somewhere, even in a city!

Green-leaved plants cover lots of land on Earth's surface.

The world looks green because of plant leaves. There are lots of different kinds of plants. The biggest group of plants are flowering plants. This includes all sorts of plants, from trees and shrubs to flowers and grasses.

Huge herds of zebra and wildebeest feed on the grass growing in Africa.

What are leaves for?

All green plants have leaves. Leaves are very important parts of the plant. They make food for the plant so it can grow. Leaves come in different shapes and sizes, but they all do this important thing.

Leaves also release a gas called **oxygen** into the air, and they feed animals such as sheep and cows.

Life on Earth

Green plants have been around for a very, very long time. In fact, scientists think they first started growing 420 million years ago! The green plants that were around then are different from the green plants on Earth today.

Leaves on flowering plants

Leaves are very important parts of a plant. The plant also needs other important parts to grow and survive. Different plant parts do different jobs. **Roots** hold the plant in the ground. They take in water and **nutrients** that the plant needs to grow. The **stem** holds the plant upright. It contains tiny tubes. Water, nutrients, and food flow in these tubes to all parts of the plant.

You can see the roots of this primrose reaching down into the soil.

Flowers and leaves

Flowers are there to make seeds. They do this by getting **pollen** from other flowers. The pollen is carried between the flowers by animals, such as bees, or by the wind. Seeds can then grow into new plants. Leaves grow from leaf **stalks**, and their job is making food for the plant.

Same parts, different plants

Although **broadleaved** trees look totally different from tiny flowers, they all have the same plant parts – roots, stems, leaves, and flowers. Tree stems are called **trunks**.

All the plants you can see here have flowers – even the trees and the grass.

Food factories

Animals, including humans, need to eat food to give them energy to grow and survive. Plants make their own food in their leaves.

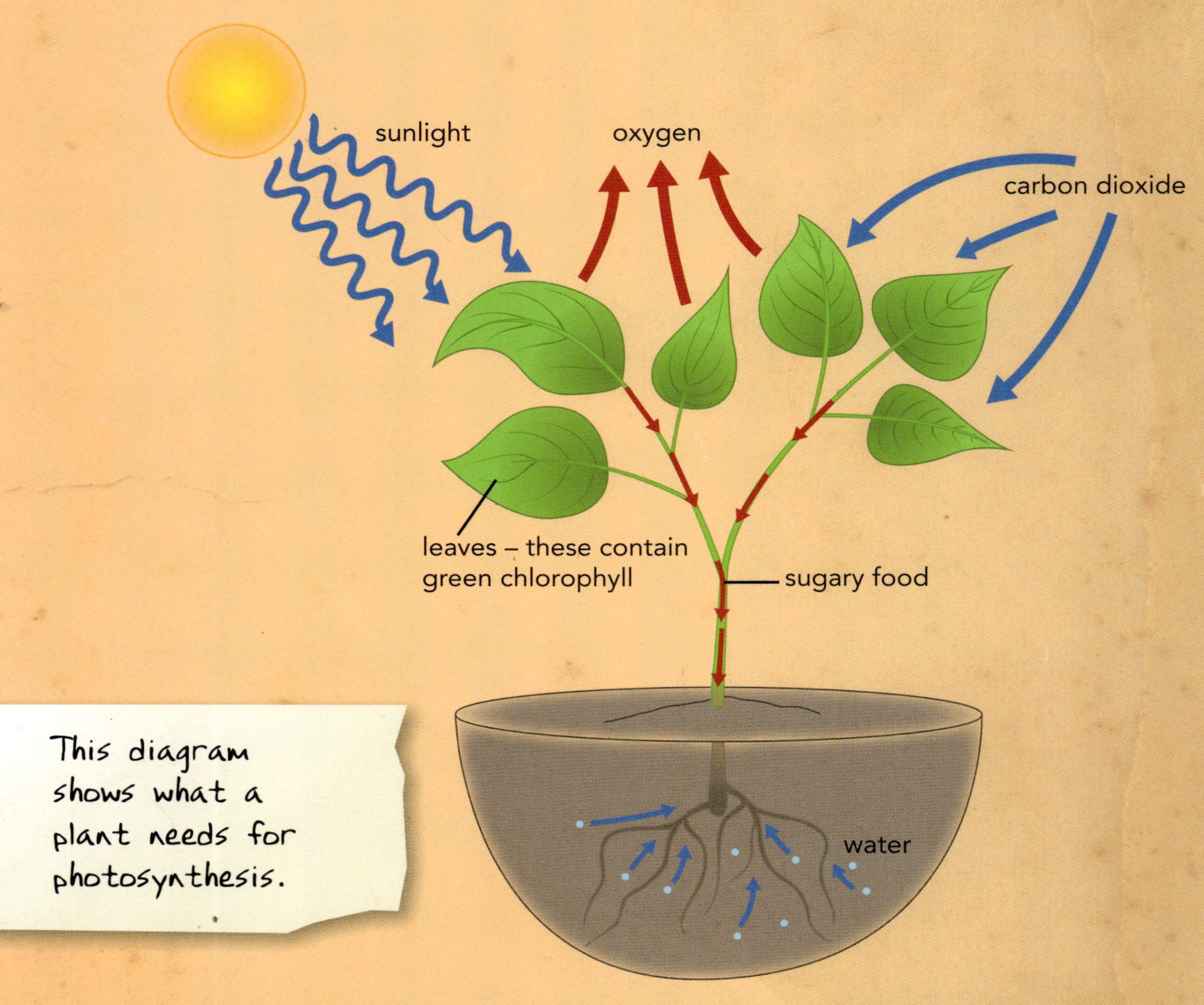

This diagram shows what a plant needs for photosynthesis.

To make food, leaves need sunlight and water. They also need a gas from the air called **carbon dioxide**. These things react with a green chemical called **chlorophyll** inside the leaves. The leaves can then make a sugary liquid that gives the plant the energy it needs. This process is called **photosynthesis**.

Giving out oxygen

When photosynthesis happens, the leaf also makes a gas called oxygen. Some of this is released into the air. Humans and other animals need to breathe oxygen to stay alive. This means that plants are especially important for life on Earth.

Moving leaves

Plants can turn their leaves so that they catch as much light as possible. If you watch a field of sunflowers over the course of a day, as the sun moves across the sky, you will see the leaves slowly turn to follow the sun.

Some plants have leaves that are not green. They still contain green chlorophyll, but they also contain other chemicals that change their colour.

Try this!

Leaves need light to make food. Try this experiment to see how a plant seeks out light.

You will need:

- two similar plants in pots
- cardboard box
- scissors
- water

1 Find two very similar plants in pots. Make sure your plants look healthy and have some leaves.

2 Cut one side out of a cardboard box just big enough to cover one of the pots. Place the box over one of the pots so that the plant is only getting light from the open side of the box. Leave the other plant on the table, uncovered.

3 Leave your plants for a week or so. Check them now and again to see if they need any water. If you water them, give each plant the same amount.

4 After a week or so, remove the box from the plant. Compare the two plants. Can you see any difference in the way that they are growing?

5 You will see that the plant that was covered by the box is leaning to one side. This is the side of the box that was open, and letting light in. The plant is leaning towards the light because it needs light to make food.

What next?

What do you think might happen to a plant and its leaves if it received no light at all? Design an experiment to test your ideas.

Water out, water in

Leaves have another important job. They help the plant to move water up from the roots to the rest of the plant.

When thick forests release water vapour it can create a misty environment.

There are tiny holes in leaves called **stomata**. These release a gas made of water, called **water vapour**, into the air. Water moves from the stem to the leaves to replace this lost water. Water moves up from the roots to replace the water in the stem.

More water please

Plant roots need to replace the water that moves up into the stem, leaves, and air. They do this by sucking water in from the soil.

When a plant's roots do not take in enough water, the plant droops over. All of its parts become soft and floppy, like a deflating balloon. When the roots take in enough water, the plant parts become tight and strong again, like a fully blown balloon.

Thirsty plants!

A large oak tree can give off about 150,000 litres (40,000 gallons) of water through its leaves every year! It needs to replace all this water through its roots.

Seed leaves and new leaves

When a plant grows from a seed, the tiny new stem pushes up through the soil. It has one or two little seed leaves already growing on it. These provide the tiny **seedling** with enough food until the plant can start growing its first true leaves. The seed leaves look different from the true leaves. The true leaves look like the leaves of the parent plant.

You can see the long, thin seed leaves on this tomato seedling. Its first true leaves are starting to grow above these.

New leaves are growing from buds along this plant's stem.

More leaves grow

After a seedling has grown its first true leaves, more leaves can grow. They grow from little **buds** called **leaf nodes** along the stem. They can also grow at the tip of the stem.

Grasses are different from many other plants because they grow new leaves only from the bottom of their stems. This means that they can survive being nibbled by animals such as deer and zebra.

Long-lived leaves

The welwitschia is a tough plant that grows in the Namib Desert in Africa. It can live for a long time – up to 2,000 years! In all this time, it grows only two leaves!

Leaf shapes

If you look around a park or garden, you will see that there are lots of different leaf shapes. Some leaves are long and thin like grass leaves. Some are large and round like magnolia leaves. Some plants such as herb Robert have feathery leaves, and others such as holly have spiky leaves.

Leaf shapes

long and thin

triangular

pointed oval

heart-shaped

oval

round

kidney-shaped

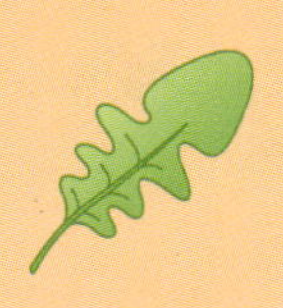

wavy

jagged

palm-shaped

spiny

Leaf edges

smooth edges

jagged edges

wavy edges

This diagram shows some of the different shapes that leaves can have. It also shows how they can be different around the edges.

Lots of rainforest trees have leaves with long, thin pointed tips at the end. These help water to run off the leaves. This is important because wet leaves can't take in as much light as dry leaves.

This elephant's ear plant has large simple leaves.

Huge leaves

The African raffia palm can grow enormous leaves, up to 25 metres (about 27 yards) long! These are compound leaves. The giant taro is a rainforest plant that grows huge simple leaves, up to 2 metres (about 2 yards) long!

One leaf, many leaves

Some plants have only one leaf growing from each leaf stalk. These are called simple leaves. Other plants have lots of smaller leaves growing from one stalk. These are called compound leaves. The laburnum tree has three leaves on each stalk. Some pea plants have 19 on each stalk!

Leaves around the stem

Leaves can grow in different ways along the stem. Some plants have leaves that grow in pairs, one from each side of the stem. Others also have pairs of leaves growing from opposite sides, but each pair grows at right angles to the pair below it. This can help the leaves to catch as much light as possible.

in pairs and opposite

in pairs, opposite, and at right angles

single leaves, opposite sides

more than two leaves, fan-shaped

This diagram shows some of the different ways that leaves grow up a plant's stem. Have a look at some plants outside to see how many different ways you can find.

Different leaf arrangements

Some plants have leaves that grow singly up the stem, not in pairs. Each one grows from the opposite side to the one below. Other plants have many leaves growing from each point on the stem. They grow in a fan around the stem.

This hebe plant has leaves that grow in pairs opposite each other, and at right angles to the pair below.

Leave them on the ground!

Some plants don't grow leaves up the length of the stem. Instead, the leaves grow only around the bottom of the stem. The dandelion has leaves like this. Only the bright yellow flower rises up on the stem.

Try this!

Use the information about leaf shapes on pages 16–17 and leaf arrangements on pages 18–19 to examine and sort different leaves.

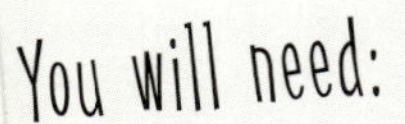

You will need:

- lots of different leaves
- scissors
- magnifying glass

1. Collect up as many different leaves as you can find. You may find some in your garden or in a park. Make sure you ask before you cut any leaves off! You may need to buy some little plants or flowers from a flower shop or garden centre.

2. Spread your leaf collection out on a table. Start looking closely at them. What shapes are they? Sort the leaves into groups that have similar shapes.

3

Now look at how the leaves are arranged on each leaf stalk. Is there only one leaf, or are there lots of leaves? Again, sort them into groups.

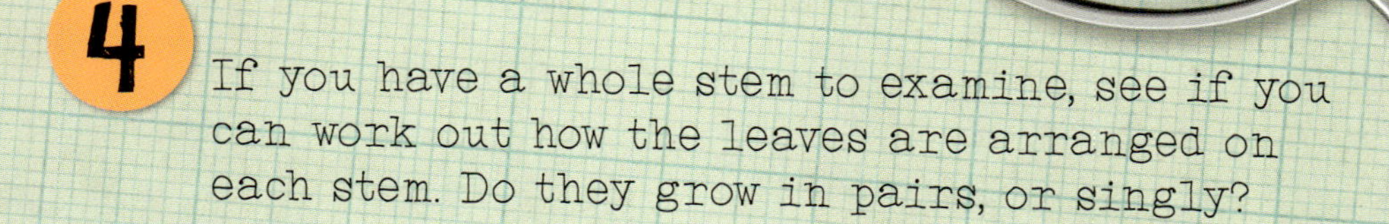

4

If you have a whole stem to examine, see if you can work out how the leaves are arranged on each stem. Do they grow in pairs, or singly?

What next?

Next time you are outside, see if you can find any leaf shapes and arrangements that are different from the ones you have examined in this activity.

Leaves in winter

All year round, the temperature in rainforest areas never gets very cold, and plants keep their leaves. This is different from other areas of the world, such as parts of Europe and North America. Here, winter temperatures can get very cold. Plants have to cope with these colder winter temperatures.

Holly trees have tough, spiny leaves that can cope with cold winter conditions. Because their leaves are smooth and shiny, snow slides easily off them.

Many plants simply die at the end of summer, after they have made seeds. The seeds grow into new plants in spring. Some **evergreen** plants have tough, waxy leaves, usually needle-shaped, that can cope with the cold weather.

Losing leaves

Plants such as trees and shrubs cope with cold winter temperatures by dropping their leaves. This helps the plant because the roots can't take up much water in cold temperatures. Losing their leaves means that the plant will stop losing water. The leaves grow again in the spring.

Autumn colours

When autumn arrives, many trees stop making green chlorophyll. This means that their leaves start turning a variety of lovely colours – yellows, oranges, reds, and browns – before falling from the tree.

Special leaves

Some leaves are specially **adapted** to do different things for the plant, as well as making food. **Tendrils** are leaves that grow like long, thin threads. They wind themselves around things to give the plant support. This helps the plant to grow tall quickly and reach more light.

This passiflora vine has tendrils to help it grow tall.

Plants such as thistles, holly, and screw pines have leaves with spikes on the ends. This stops animals from eating them. Nettle leaves are covered with tiny sharp needles. When animals brush past or try to bite them, the needles are broken off and a stinging chemical is released.

Catching animals

Some plants have leaves designed to catch animals! Sundew leaves have little hairs covered in a sticky goo. Insects stick to this goo and the leaves curl over to trap them. Venus fly-traps have special hinged leaves with teeth around the edges. These close shut when insects land on them.

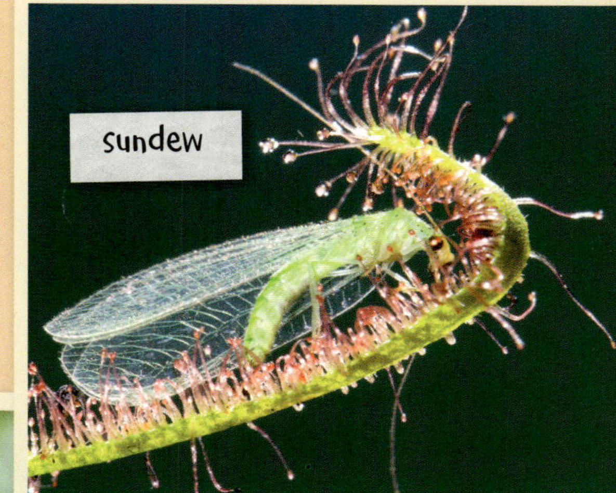
sundew

Venus fly-trap

Plants catch animals to get nutrients from their bodies. They digest the animals a bit like your stomach digests food.

Pitcher plants

Pitcher plants grow large jug-like pitchers at the ends of their leaves. Insects that land on the edge of the pitcher slide off and into a liquid inside. They can't climb back up the slippery walls to escape.

Leaves around the world

Plants can grow in all sorts of places around the world. Some have adaptations to help them. In rivers and ponds, some plants have leaves that stick up above the surface, or float. This means they can catch sunlight and make food. Plants with leaves underwater have thin, feathery leaves that are not damaged by water flowing past them.

The giant water lily has huge leaves that float on the surface of the water.

Hot and cold

In deserts, the leaves of cactus plants are shaped into sharp spines. This stops them from losing water, and also protects them from animals. Other desert plants have small, thick, fleshy leaves covered in wax. This also stops them from losing too much water.

This desert plant has lots of small, thick, fleshy leaves that have a thin coating of wax.

Plants in cold places have small leaves that grow low to the ground. This keeps them out of cold winds.

Cozy blanket

A plant called the giant lobelia grows on the high slopes of Mount Kenya in Africa. During the very cold nights, the hairy leaves fold down to protect the delicate flowers from the freezing air.

Leaves and us

Leaves are what we imagine when we think of green spaces such as fields, parks, gardens, and forests. They are the food factories of the world. They make food that animals can eat. Other animals can then eat these animals.

These cows are getting energy from grass. They use this energy to grow and to make milk. We can drink the milk and eat the meat from the cow.

Plants are called **producers**, because they produce their own food. They are at the start of all of Earth's **food chains**.

Tea leaves like these have been harvested and traded around the world for thousands of years.

Using leaves

We don't just use leaves to eat. Some leaves contain useful chemicals. For example, a chemical in foxglove leaves can be used in heart medicines. Aloe vera leaves are used to make make-up and skin creams. We make tea using tea leaves, and we use herb leaves for different flavours in cooking.

Leafy symbols

The maple leaf is a symbol of Canada. Other leaves have been used as symbols in the past: oak leaves for faith, bay leaves for healing, and ivy leaves for friendship.

Glossary

adapt change over time to suit the environment

broadleaved tree with flat, wide leaves rather than thin needles. Trees with needles are called conifers.

bud swelling on a plant that can grow into new parts, such as leaves or a flower

carbon dioxide gas with no colour or smell that is found in the air

chlorophyll green substance in plant leaves and stems that traps sunlight for photosynthesis

evergreen tree, bush, or other plant with leaves that remain on the plant and stay green throughout the year

food chain series of living things where each one is eaten by the next

leaf node type of bud that leaves grow from

nutrient chemical that helps plants to live and grow

oxygen gas with no colour or smell that makes up about one-fifth of air. Most living things need oxygen.

photosynthesis process by which plants use water, sunlight, and carbon dioxide to make food for themselves

pollen fine powder made in plant flowers. It is used by plants to fertilize flowers to make seeds.

producer living thing that makes food for itself and does not have to eat other things

roots parts of plants that usually grow underground. They take water and nutrients from the soil, and hold the plant in the ground.

seedling very young plant that has grown from a seed

stalk plant part that grows from the stem and supports a leaf or a flower

stem main part of a plant that supports the branches, leaves, and flowers

stomata tiny holes in plant leaves. Water and gases can pass in and out of stomata.

tendril special leaf or part of the stem that grows long and attaches to things to support the plant

trunk thick, hard stem of a tree

water vapour water in the form of gas

Find out more

Books

Leaves (See How Plants Grow), Nicola Edwards (Wayland, 2009)

Plants (Wildlife Watchers), Terry Jennings (QED, 2010)

Zoom! The Invisible World of Plants, Camilla de la Bedoyere (QED, 2012)

Websites

www.bbc.co.uk/learningzone/clips/photosynthesis-in-plants/67.html
This website has a video all about photosynthesis.

www.bbc.co.uk/nature/plants
This website has lots of information about plants. There are also some amazing film clips of plants all around the world.

www.bgfl.org/bgfl/custom/resources_ftp/client_ftp/ks2/science/s_plants/index.htm Have a look at this website to find out more about how plants work.

www.rhs.org.uk/Children/For-kids/Mostest-plants Go to this web page to find out interesting facts about the tallest tree, smelliest flower, and speediest seed!

www.sciencekids.co.nz/gamesactivities/lifecycles.html
There are interactive activities on this website where you can test what you know about plant parts, and find out more.

Places to visit

The Natural History Museum in London has hundreds of displays and activities. You can learn about how plants and animals have changed over time, and how scientists work to discover all about the natural world.

The Royal Botanic Gardens in Kew in London has plants from all over the world.

The Eden Project in Cornwall is a series of huge domed greenhouses, one of which contains a rainforest! There are fun activities and amazing things to learn about plants.

Go for a walk in your local nature park! Spend time looking closely at all the different leaves you can see.

Index